JEAN CRAIGHEAD GEORGE

The WOLVES *Are* BACK

PAINTINGS BY WENDELL MINOR

Dutton Children's Books

ACKNOWLEDGMENTS

The artist wishes to thank photographers Thomas D. Mangelsen, Cathy Wise, and Charlie Craighead for providing valuable photo reference sources for the paintings in this book, and to the wolves at The Wolf Conservation Center in South Salem, New York, who became the models for some of the paintings. Great thanks also to Charlie Craighead for guiding the author and artist on a tour of the Lamar Valley, and very special thanks to Jean Craighead George for being a true and constant source of inspiration to the artist.

DUTTON CHILDREN'S BOOKS · A division of Penguin Young Readers Group · Published by the Penguin Group

Penguin Group (USA) Inc., 375 Hudson Street, New York, New York 10014, U.S.A. · Penguin Group (Canada), 90 Eglinton Avenue East, Suite 700, Toronto, Ontario, Canada M4P 2Y3 (a division of Pearson Penguin Canada Inc.) · Penguin Books Ltd, 80 Strand, London WC2R 0RL, England · Penguin Ireland, 25 St Stephen's Green, Dublin 2, Ireland (a division of Penguin Books Ltd) · Penguin Group (Australia), 250 Camberwell Road, Camberwell, Victoria 3124, Australia (a division of Pearson Australia Group Pty Ltd) · Penguin Books India Pvt Ltd, 11 Community Centre, Panchsheel Park, New Delhi - 110 017, India · Penguin Group (NZ), 67 Apollo Drive, Rosedale, North Shore 0632, New Zealand (a division of Pearson New Zealand Ltd) · Penguin Books (South Africa) (Pty) Ltd, 24 Sturdee Avenue, Rosebank, Johannesburg 2196, South Africa

Penguin Books Ltd, Registered Offices: 80 Strand, London WC2R 0RL, England

Library of Congress Cataloging-in-Publication Data

George, Jean Craighead, date.

The wolves are back / Jean Craighead George ; Illustrated by Wendell Minor.—1st ed.   p. cm.

ISBN 978-0-525-47947-5 (hardcover)

1. Wolves—Juvenile literature. 2. Wolves—Reintroduction—Yellowstone National Park—Juvenile literature. I. Minor, Wendell, ill. II. Title.

QL737.C22G449 2008   599.773—dc22   2007017064

Published in the United States by Dutton Children's Books, a division of Penguin Young Readers Group

345 Hudson Street, New York, New York 10014 · www.penguin.com/youngreaders

Manufactured in China · First Edition · 10 9 8 7 6 5 4 3 2 1

To Ai Li

JEAN CRAIGHEAD GEORGE

To all the people who made
 it possible for the wolves to
return to Yellowstone

WENDELL MINOR

The wolf pup pricked up his ears, pattered out of the den, and followed his father down the slope. They jogged through the lush grasses to the bank of the Lamar River in Yellowstone National Park. There they came upon the carcass of an elk their pack had felled.

The wolves were back!

The pup watched his father eat. Then he, too, tore off a bite. Two ravens stuffed themselves. A golden eagle carried off food for her eaglets. A grizzly bear sat nearby waiting for the wolves to leave so she could eat in peace. Three magpies snatched quick bites. Mice chewed on calcium-filled antlers. Two sexton beetles buried a piece of meat to eat later. The valley was sharing food again.

The wolves were back.

Where had they been?

Shot. Every one.

Many years ago the directors of the national parks decided that only the gentle animals should grace the beautiful wilderness. Rangers, hunters, and ranchers were told to shoot every wolf they saw. They did. By 1926, there were no more wolves in the forty-eight states. No voices howled. The thrilling chorus of the wilderness was silenced.

The wolves were gone.

The deer, elk, antelope—the gentle animals—looked beautiful in photographs.
They wandered in tranquil herds. Peace reigned in the American wilderness.
The wolves were gone.

Time passed. Visitors to wild America yearned to hear wolves. When they learned that no wolf had ever attacked a person in North America, they urged that the wolves be returned to their home.

In 1995, ten adult wolves were brought down from Canada and set free in Yellowstone National Park. They dug dens and bore puppies. First there were three packs, then there were five. In six years there were twenty-one packs. They howled and sang to each other. Hikers stopped and marveled at the sound.

The wolves were back.

The pup who had followed his father to eat heard a Vesper sparrow sing.
This songster had not been in the Lamar Valley for almost a century.

The vast elk herds had eaten the grasses the little bird needed for food and nesting material. When the wolves returned, they frightened the elk up into the mountains. The grasses grew tall.

The sparrows raised babies and sang.

The wolves were back.

The wolf pup heard a flycatcher call. The Lamar Valley had not heard this flycatcher while the bison were there. Bison break and trample young trees to keep back the forest so there will be grass. Now the wolves hunted the bison and drove them back from the river. Without the bison, the aspens grew. With the trees restored, there were limbs for the flycatcher to perch on. They sat there and sang.

The wolves were back.

When grass and aspen were deep along the riverbanks, erosion was stopped. Willows grew. Beavers arrived and felled the willows, ate the bark, and made dams with the logs. The dams formed ponds. Waterbirds, fish, and frogs flocked to the ponds. Dragonflies zoomed above them.

The pup peered ahead. In front of him sat one of the few coyotes the wolves had not killed when they first arrived in the valley. After the wolves thinned out the coyotes, the number of ground squirrels that the coyotes fed upon increased. Ground squirrels were the badgers' main food. Badgers moved back into the valley now rich with ground squirrels. The badgers ate well and dug tunnels for homes.

The wolves were back.

The grizzly bears shared the wolf kills and had two and even three big, fat healthy cubs.

The wolf pup with his father ate until his stomach was round and then followed his father back to their den. They walked through gardens of wildflowers. The wolves had scared the mountain sheep that chew the flowers to the ground up into the rocky cliffs.

Flowers filled the valley. Bees and butterflies that fed on the flowers
returned. Warblers sang. Hummingbirds brightened the valley. Like pieces
in a kaleidoscope, the broken parts of the wilderness were tumbling into place.
The wolves were back.

The pup grew up. He was taught to hunt by his father and mother.
He helped take care of the next litter of puppies, then he left home.

The young male went south where he met a mate from the Yellowstone Delta Pack. They trotted side by side into the Teton wilderness and dug a den along the Snake River. They scared the elk away. They scattered the bison. They frightened the sheep up into the cliffs.

The grasses grew tall; the riverbank stopped eroding. Willow and aspen trees flourished. Beavers built ponds. Birds sang. Flowers bloomed.

The wilderness is in balance again.

The wolves are back.

Sources

The artist had the great privilege of spending time with Jean Craighead George, who shared her vast knowledge on the subject of wolves. In addition, the artist used the following sources:

Ballantine, Richard. Photographs by Jim Dutcher. *The Sawtooth Wolves*. Bearsville, NY: Rufus Publications, 1996.

Dutcher, Jim and Jamie. *Living with Wolves*. Seattle, WA: Mountaineers Books, 2005.

Ferguson, Gary. *The Yellowstone Wolf*. Helena, MT: Falcon Press, 1966.

Mech, L. David. *The Way of the Wolf*. Stillwater, MN: Voyageur Press, 1991.

White, P. J. and R. A. Garrott. *ScienceDirect*, vol. 125, issue 2, September, 2005, pp. 141–152.

www.mangelsen.com

www.wisenaturephotos.com

www.nywolf.org